Grace Through Hardship

Linda Kaye Randall
LKR Unlimited Opportunities LLC
440 Monticello Avenue STE 1802 #169339
Norfolk, VA 23510-2670

Publisher: LKR Unlimited Opportunities, LLC
Editing & Book Formatting Services: V.I.P. Coaching & Consulting Services

First Edition
ISBN: 979-8-9995168-1-7

For inquiries about permissions, speaking engagements, or bulk order purchases, please contact linda@lindakayerandall.com

From My Heart to Yours

I would like to extend my compassion to those of you going through some type of health journey personally or with a loved one. I hope this journal provides a place for you to express yourself in ways that you may not be able or willing to share with others within your circle. I know that journaling helped me with my journey. This is your safe place to document and release whatever you are keeping locked inside. This process helps you to process the situation and I personally believe it is essential for maintaining some level of equilibrium as you walk the road that has been laid out before you.

God Bless you and yours as the journey unfolds,
Linda

Checkout the visitation & procedure guide that provides visitation preparation checklists, ideas for activities, a section to record doctor/staff consultations and to log aspects that impact the feelings and overall quality of life issues for overall well-being.

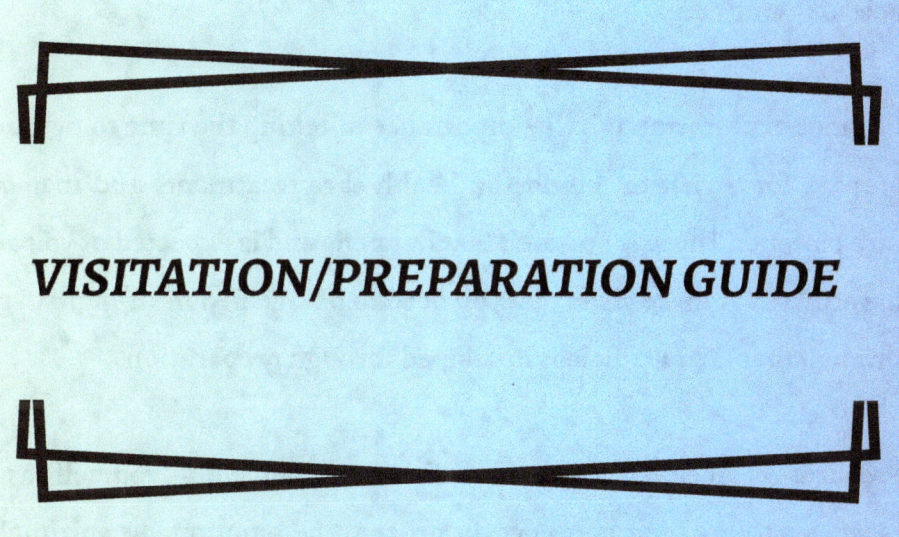

VISITATION/PREPARATION GUIDE

The best preparation is to have in place all legal documents for estate planning, health related decisions and power of attorney needs before you start treatments, have surgery or start to have memory issues. If not in place it can place an unforeseen tremendous burden on your loved ones if you are not capable of making decisions or pass away . If you are still healthy and can manage it financially, long-term care insurance is well worth the investment. The cost is reduced significantly the sooner you get it and will provide a blanket of financial security in the event you need ongoing care.

I cannot express enough the importance of taking the time to properly prepare for a visit to the doctor, health care treatments and memory care patients. There is so much that happens and is expected of you and the afflicted at these visits that you need to be shielded in strength to get through them. Your shield is developed through preparation.

Preparation includes, first and foremost, allowing yourself as a caregiver to do what you need in order to be emotionally, spiritually, mentally and physically able to perform the tasks required of you in a rational, efficient and safe manner. This will differ by person but will likely involve a routine or ritual of one or more of the following: rest, focus, worship, meditation, sleep, healthy eating and hydration, exercise, social interaction, hobbies, support groups, therapy, etc. Please make sure you allow for your self-care in this journey. Your ability to sustain any long-term caregiving for an illness requires you to be healthy.

VISITATION PREPARATION GUIDE / CHECKLIST

1. Create a space for yourself to be alone if you are living with others, so that you can be by yourself to process everything as needed. Where is your space?

2. Create a space to use for preparation of items for appointments, treatments and visits, so that you have a dedicated area and can have items handy for movement from one carry bag to another as needed. Define your space:

3. Duplicate some items like tissues, snacks, etc. so you don't have to always move things around if each event requires a lot of specialized items, but you also need basic supplies. What are your items?

4. It is important that if you have to wait or be in treatments for a long period of time to have a prepared healthy lunch, snacks, drinks, etc. What is your favorite allowed go-to foods?

5. Prepare for your and the patient's entertainment during the visits, crossword books, music lists with earbuds, reading books/magazines, crochet/knit, etc. What interests you and your loved one?

6. For memory care visits you need to plan even more for how you will interact and have a backup plan in case the visit is not going as you hope - memory books, crafts, balloon toss, storytelling, celebratory items or food, etc. Be willing to go with the flow and be imaginative as that can be the saving grace in your time with your loved one. What are your loved one's favorite things? What do they need to work on (physical or mental) exercises?

7. What supplies need to be replenished: medical supplies, grooming items, clothing, reading material, writing material, if permitted (note: pens, pencils can be weaponized and may not be permitted), slippers, towels, deodorizers, hangers, hampers, shower chairs, other furniture requirements, wall hangings, family photos, unbreakable handheld mirrors, tv's or music players if allowed, specialty items, etc. What are key items you know you need to bring regularly?

8. Make notes for what occurred during the visit and any items/questions/concerns that you need to pursue or bring next time.

Questions/Concerns for Preparation for Doctor and Treatment visits:

1. Talk about the duration in days, weeks, months of the treatment plan

2. How long and often are treatments required? Each day, week, month, etc.

3. Side Effects that can be expected – understand the uncommon ones as well, you could be the minority percentage

4. Transportation concerns

5. Who is available for support during your visits (if you attend by yourself, who is your emergency point of contact)

6. Quality of life issues (really research what is being suggested for you to see if the plan fits in with how you want to live your life)

7. Ensure your legal paperwork is in order (wills, living wills, advanced medical directives, Power of Attorney, do not resuscitate, trusts, etc.) This cannot be under emphasized – be prepared.

8. Rehabilitation requirements – understand the known requirements and length, so barring any unforeseen issues, you can have a facility already picked out and scheduled for any post treatment/surgery needs.

9. Do research on the hospital / treatment facility to ensure it fits your needs and specializes in the care you require.

10. Do some financial planning for any missed income during your recovery

11. Who will be staying with you during recovery, if needed

12. What are your dietary restrictions?11. Sometimes it is temporary, sometimes it is permanent. Understand your post illness needs to remain healthy.

13. What medical equipment, special needs will you require. This is important as you may have to rearrange your living environment or schedule to accommodate on going life sustaining issues, temporarily or on a permanent basis.

14. How much does your insurance cover for pre, during, post and ongoing needs for treatments, surgery, rehabilitation, recovery and ongoing health maintenance?

15. What are your spiritual, emotional and mental support needs during these periods of time? Ensure you have a plan in place to have those needs met and that your loved ones understand your desires.

16. Provide a framework if not a prearranged plan for any funeral and bequeath wishes, just in case.

There are likely other items that your particular situation may require, but these are the basics.

Proper planning allows for the patient and loved ones to understand and process more of the situation they are going to be experiencing, potentially reducing the level of stress.

Quick Start Journaling

This journal is specially designed to help people that need a quick easy way to capture their spiritual, emotional, mental and physical condition at any given time or day. People in crisis/survivor mode go through a wide range of emotions, sometimes within minutes of each other or all at once. Allowing yourself or a loved one a place to log those feelings provides a unique type of release for the stress they are experiencing. Please use this journal as often as needed and carry it with you to help pass the time while you are in a period of waiting, wanting to release your thoughts and energy or need to capture notes for future reference.

The basic design of this journal provides a quick reference guide for over 200 words linked to expressing feelings. Use the guide to pick out as many of the feelings you are experiencing that you want to focus on for that entry. Pick the top five otherwise you could never stop writing! This journal also provides 20 prompting questions to help you get started.

Next give a brief synopsis of what event triggered the feeling, if there was one. Sometimes we just feel and that is o.k., you can still journal about it.

Then as your time permits expound on your feelings, thoughts, wishes, prayers, conversations and events in more detail. This is an experience that provides a sense of well-being. It provides a safe place to release anything you need to without judgement. It is amazing how journaling allows our minds to become clearer in order to process our reality in a more objective healthy manner.

This journal doesn't have to be only for feelings associated with going through a health crisis. Unfortunately, most of us will experience multiple stressful situations at one time, so this journal allows anything impacting you to be captured. After all, every event impacts your overall feelings and well-being.

POTENTIAL FEELING WORDS

ADORED

AMAZED

AMBIGUOUS

AMBITIOUS

AMBIVILANT

AMUSED

ANGELIC

ANGER

ANGST

ANNOYED

ANXIOUS

APATHETIC

APPRECIATED

APPRECIATIVE

BEDAZZLED

BEMUSED

BERATED

BEWILDERED

BLESSED

BORED

BROKEN

CAUTIOUS

CENTERED

CHEERFUL

CHRISTIAN

CONSCIENSIOUS

COURTEOUS

CRAZY

CREATIVE

CURIOUS

DAZED

DELIBERATE

DEPRESSED

DESERVING

DESOLATE

DESPERATE

DESPONDANT

DISCERNING

DISPARE

DISTRAUGHT

DROWNING

DRUNK

DUMPED ON

EMOTIONAL

EMPATHETIC

EMPATHY

ENCOURAGED

ENGAGED

ENTERTAINED

ENTHUSIASTIC

FAILURE

FAKE

FALSE

FEMININE

FORLORNE

FRACTURED

FRAIL

FRAZZLED

FREEDOM

FRUGAL

FRUSTRATED

FUNCTIONAL

GODLINESS

GOODNESS

GRACIOUS

GRATEFUL

GRATITUDE

HAPPY

HATEFUL

POTENTIAL FEELING WORDS

HAUGHTY	KINKY	MINDFUL
HEALTHY	LETHARGIC	MINIMIZED
HEARD	LAZY	MIRACULOUS
HONEST	LEFT	MIXED UP
HOPEFUL	LIFTED	OBJECTIVE
HORRENDOUS	LIVELY	OBJECTIFIED
HORRIFIED	LONELY	OBLIGATED
HUMBLE	LONGING	OBLIGED
HUMOROUS	LOOPY	OBSESSED
HUNGRY	LOST	OBSTINATE
IDLE	LOUD	ODD
IGNORANT	LOUSY	OLD
ILLUMINATED	LOVELY	ONEROUS
INNOCENT	MAD	OPPRESSED
INSIGHTFUL	MAGICAL	ORDINARY
IRKED	MAGNIFICINT	ORNERY
JEALOUS	MAJESTIC	PETTY
JOYFUL	MANLY	PHYSICAL
JUDGED	MARVELOUS	PIUS
JUDGEMENTAL	MATCHED	PLEASANT
KEPT	MAUDLIN	PLEASED
KIND	MESSED UP	PLEASURE
KINGLY	MESSY	POMPOUS

POTENTIAL FEELING WORDS

PRAISED	SERIOUS	TIRED
PRAYERFUL	SEXY	TOLERANT
PRETTY	SILENCED	TOUCHED
PREYED UPON	SILENT	TOUGH
PRIDE	SOBER	TRAMPLED ON
PRIDEFUL	SOULESS	TRAPPED
PROVIDED FOR	SOULFULL	TRAUMATIZED
PTIFUL	SPIRITUAL	TREMBLING
PURE	STRIPED	TRIED
PUTRID	SYMPATHETIC	UNADORED
QUEENLY	SYMPATHY	UNAPPRECIATED
QUESTIONABLE	TANGIBLE	UNDONE
RANKOR	TEARFUL	UNIFIED
RANTING	TEARS	UNIQUE
RAUCOUS	TERRIFIC	UNIVERSAL
REGULATED	TERRIFIED	UNLOVED
RELUNCTANT	TERROR	UNTETHERED
RIDICULOUS	TESTED	VERIFIED
RIGHT	TESTIFIED	VOLUMTUOUS
ROUGH	TETHERED	VULNERABLE
SAD	TIMID	WANDERING
SASSY	TINGLY	WANTING
SCATTERED	TINY	WASTEFUL

POTENTIAL FEELING WORDS

WEALTHY
WHIMSICAL
WISHFUL
WONDERFUL
XRAYED
YEARNING
YOUNG
YOUTHFUL
ZEALOUS

It's okay to not be okay! ♥

you are NOT ALONE in this.

Stop BREATHE & THINK

find Joy in the JOURNEY

One Step At A Time

Just Take Deep Breaths

it's okay to feel

your feelings

STAY Hopeful

<u>Prompting Questions /Thoughts</u>

Begin your journal journey. You decide what, when, how much, who and where to write.

- *Where are you when you are writing this entry?*

- *Why are you there?*

- *Are you there for yourself or for someone else?*

- *What is your role in the process?*

- *How does that make you feel?*

- *How long have you been dealing with the issues you are writing about?*

- *Do you have multiple issues going on at once?*

- *How many do you want to write about?*

- *Sometimes the things we think are insignificant are the items we need to express.*

- *Did you do something that you need to resolve?*

- *How are your feelings and/or the situation impacting your life?*
- *Are your relationships being impacted? How? This can be positive or negative or not at all.*
- *Is there anything you can do differently?*
- *Did you properly prepare for your visit or procedure?*
- *Can you ask for help? Will you? Who would you ask?*
- *Has this impacted your spiritual awareness?*
- *How is it impacting your financial security?*
- *Noting the timeframe between entries can really make you revisit and think about what you write.*
- *Are you writing to release your feelings or to document the journey from many angles?*
- *Intent of the journal five or more years from now?*

*Jot down your specific questions you would like
to ask yourself before writing below:*

DAY/DATE: DAY #:

TOP FIVE FEELING WORDS FOR THIS JOURNAL
ENTRY:

WHERE AND WHAT PROMPTED THESE
FEELINGS (BRIEFLY)?

ELABORATE AS MUCH AS YOU WISH ON ANY
TOPIC:

DAY/DATE: DAY #:

TOP FIVE FEELING WORDS FOR THIS JOURNAL
ENTRY:

WHERE AND WHAT PROMPTED THESE
FEELINGS (BRIEFLY)?

ELABORATE AS MUCH AS YOU WISH ON ANY
TOPIC:

DAY/DATE: DAY #:

TOP FIVE FEELING WORDS FOR THIS JOURNAL
ENTRY:

WHERE AND WHAT PROMPTED THESE
FEELINGS (BRIEFLY)?

ELABORATE AS MUCH AS YOU WISH ON ANY
TOPIC:

DAY/DATE: DAY #:

TOP FIVE FEELING WORDS FOR THIS JOURNAL
ENTRY:

WHERE AND WHAT PROMPTED THESE
FEELINGS (BRIEFLY)?

ELABORATE AS MUCH AS YOU WISH ON ANY
TOPIC:

DAY/DATE: DAY #:

TOP FIVE FEELING WORDS FOR THIS JOURNAL ENTRY:

WHERE AND WHAT PROMPTED THESE FEELINGS (BRIEFLY)?

ELABORATE AS MUCH AS YOU WISH ON ANY TOPIC:

DAY/DATE: DAY #:

TOP FIVE FEELING WORDS FOR THIS JOURNAL
ENTRY:

WHERE AND WHAT PROMPTED THESE
FEELINGS (BRIEFLY)?

ELABORATE AS MUCH AS YOU WISH ON ANY
TOPIC:

DAY/DATE: **DAY #:**

TOP FIVE FEELING WORDS FOR THIS JOURNAL ENTRY:

WHERE AND WHAT PROMPTED THESE FEELINGS (BRIEFLY)?

ELABORATE AS MUCH AS YOU WISH ON ANY TOPIC:

DAY/DATE: DAY #:

TOP FIVE FEELING WORDS FOR THIS JOURNAL
ENTRY:

WHERE AND WHAT PROMPTED THESE
FEELINGS (BRIEFLY)?

ELABORATE AS MUCH AS YOU WISH ON ANY
TOPIC:

DAY/DATE: DAY #:

TOP FIVE FEELING WORDS FOR THIS JOURNAL
ENTRY:

WHERE AND WHAT PROMPTED THESE
FEELINGS (BRIEFLY)?

ELABORATE AS MUCH AS YOU WISH ON ANY
TOPIC:

DAY/DATE: DAY #:

TOP FIVE FEELING WORDS FOR THIS JOURNAL
ENTRY:

WHERE AND WHAT PROMPTED THESE
FEELINGS (BRIEFLY)?

ELABORATE AS MUCH AS YOU WISH ON ANY
TOPIC:

DAY/DATE: DAY #:

TOP FIVE FEELING WORDS FOR THIS JOURNAL
ENTRY:

WHERE AND WHAT PROMPTED THESE
FEELINGS (BRIEFLY)?

ELABORATE AS MUCH AS YOU WISH ON ANY
TOPIC:

DAY/DATE: DAY #:

TOP FIVE FEELING WORDS FOR THIS JOURNAL
ENTRY:

WHERE AND WHAT PROMPTED THESE
FEELINGS (BRIEFLY)?

ELABORATE AS MUCH AS YOU WISH ON ANY
TOPIC:

DAY/DATE: DAY #:

TOP FIVE FEELING WORDS FOR THIS JOURNAL
ENTRY:

WHERE AND WHAT PROMPTED THESE
FEELINGS (BRIEFLY)?

ELABORATE AS MUCH AS YOU WISH ON ANY
TOPIC:

DAY/DATE: DAY #:

TOP FIVE FEELING WORDS FOR THIS JOURNAL
ENTRY:

WHERE AND WHAT PROMPTED THESE
FEELINGS (BRIEFLY)?

ELABORATE AS MUCH AS YOU WISH ON ANY
TOPIC:

DAY/DATE: DAY #:

TOP FIVE FEELING WORDS FOR THIS JOURNAL
ENTRY:

WHERE AND WHAT PROMPTED THESE
FEELINGS (BRIEFLY)?

ELABORATE AS MUCH AS YOU WISH ON ANY
TOPIC:

DAY/DATE: DAY #:

TOP FIVE FEELING WORDS FOR THIS JOURNAL
ENTRY:

WHERE AND WHAT PROMPTED THESE
FEELINGS (BRIEFLY)?

ELABORATE AS MUCH AS YOU WISH ON ANY
TOPIC:

DAY/DATE: DAY #:

TOP FIVE FEELING WORDS FOR THIS JOURNAL
ENTRY:

WHERE AND WHAT PROMPTED THESE
FEELINGS (BRIEFLY)?

ELABORATE AS MUCH AS YOU WISH ON ANY
TOPIC:

DAY/DATE: DAY #:

TOP FIVE FEELING WORDS FOR THIS JOURNAL
ENTRY:

WHERE AND WHAT PROMPTED THESE
FEELINGS (BRIEFLY)?

ELABORATE AS MUCH AS YOU WISH ON ANY
TOPIC:

DAY/DATE: DAY #:

TOP FIVE FEELING WORDS FOR THIS JOURNAL
ENTRY:

WHERE AND WHAT PROMPTED THESE
FEELINGS (BRIEFLY)?

ELABORATE AS MUCH AS YOU WISH ON ANY
TOPIC:

DAY/DATE: DAY #:

TOP FIVE FEELING WORDS FOR THIS JOURNAL
ENTRY:

WHERE AND WHAT PROMPTED THESE
FEELINGS (BRIEFLY)?

ELABORATE AS MUCH AS YOU WISH ON ANY
TOPIC:

DAY/DATE: **DAY #:**

TOP FIVE FEELING WORDS FOR THIS JOURNAL ENTRY:

WHERE AND WHAT PROMPTED THESE FEELINGS (BRIEFLY)?

ELABORATE AS MUCH AS YOU WISH ON ANY TOPIC:

DAY/DATE: DAY #:

TOP FIVE FEELING WORDS FOR THIS JOURNAL
ENTRY:

WHERE AND WHAT PROMPTED THESE
FEELINGS (BRIEFLY)?

ELABORATE AS MUCH AS YOU WISH ON ANY
TOPIC:

DAY/DATE: DAY #:

TOP FIVE FEELING WORDS FOR THIS JOURNAL
ENTRY:

WHERE AND WHAT PROMPTED THESE
FEELINGS (BRIEFLY)?

ELABORATE AS MUCH AS YOU WISH ON ANY
TOPIC:

DAY/DATE: DAY #:

TOP FIVE FEELING WORDS FOR THIS JOURNAL
ENTRY:

WHERE AND WHAT PROMPTED THESE
FEELINGS (BRIEFLY)?

ELABORATE AS MUCH AS YOU WISH ON ANY
TOPIC:

DAY/DATE: DAY #:

TOP FIVE FEELING WORDS FOR THIS JOURNAL
ENTRY:

WHERE AND WHAT PROMPTED THESE
FEELINGS (BRIEFLY)?

ELABORATE AS MUCH AS YOU WISH ON ANY
TOPIC:

DAY/DATE: DAY #:

TOP FIVE FEELING WORDS FOR THIS JOURNAL
ENTRY:

WHERE AND WHAT PROMPTED THESE
FEELINGS (BRIEFLY)?

ELABORATE AS MUCH AS YOU WISH ON ANY
TOPIC:

DAY/DATE: DAY #:

TOP FIVE FEELING WORDS FOR THIS JOURNAL ENTRY:

WHERE AND WHAT PROMPTED THESE FEELINGS (BRIEFLY)?

ELABORATE AS MUCH AS YOU WISH ON ANY TOPIC:

DAY/DATE: DAY #:

TOP FIVE FEELING WORDS FOR THIS JOURNAL
ENTRY:

WHERE AND WHAT PROMPTED THESE
FEELINGS (BRIEFLY)?

ELABORATE AS MUCH AS YOU WISH ON ANY
TOPIC:

DAY/DATE: DAY #:

TOP FIVE FEELING WORDS FOR THIS JOURNAL
ENTRY:

WHERE AND WHAT PROMPTED THESE
FEELINGS (BRIEFLY)?

ELABORATE AS MUCH AS YOU WISH ON ANY
TOPIC:

DAY/DATE: DAY #:

TOP FIVE FEELING WORDS FOR THIS JOURNAL
ENTRY:

WHERE AND WHAT PROMPTED THESE
FEELINGS (BRIEFLY)?

ELABORATE AS MUCH AS YOU WISH ON ANY
TOPIC:

DAY/DATE: DAY #:

TOP FIVE FEELING WORDS FOR THIS JOURNAL
ENTRY:

WHERE AND WHAT PROMPTED THESE
FEELINGS (BRIEFLY)?

ELABORATE AS MUCH AS YOU WISH ON ANY
TOPIC:

DAY/DATE: DAY #:

TOP FIVE FEELING WORDS FOR THIS JOURNAL
ENTRY:

WHERE AND WHAT PROMPTED THESE
FEELINGS (BRIEFLY)?

ELABORATE AS MUCH AS YOU WISH ON ANY
TOPIC:

DAY/DATE: DAY #:

TOP FIVE FEELING WORDS FOR THIS JOURNAL
ENTRY:

WHERE AND WHAT PROMPTED THESE
FEELINGS (BRIEFLY)?

ELABORATE AS MUCH AS YOU WISH ON ANY
TOPIC:

DAY/DATE: DAY #:

TOP FIVE FEELING WORDS FOR THIS JOURNAL
ENTRY:

WHERE AND WHAT PROMPTED THESE
FEELINGS (BRIEFLY)?

ELABORATE AS MUCH AS YOU WISH ON ANY
TOPIC:

DAY/DATE: DAY #:

TOP FIVE FEELING WORDS FOR THIS JOURNAL
ENTRY:

WHERE AND WHAT PROMPTED THESE
FEELINGS (BRIEFLY)?

ELABORATE AS MUCH AS YOU WISH ON ANY
TOPIC:

DAY/DATE: DAY #:

TOP FIVE FEELING WORDS FOR THIS JOURNAL
ENTRY:

WHERE AND WHAT PROMPTED THESE
FEELINGS (BRIEFLY)?

ELABORATE AS MUCH AS YOU WISH ON ANY
TOPIC:

DAY/DATE: **DAY #:**

TOP FIVE FEELING WORDS FOR THIS JOURNAL ENTRY:

WHERE AND WHAT PROMPTED THESE FEELINGS (BRIEFLY)?

ELABORATE AS MUCH AS YOU WISH ON ANY TOPIC:

DAY/DATE: DAY #:

TOP FIVE FEELING WORDS FOR THIS JOURNAL
ENTRY:

WHERE AND WHAT PROMPTED THESE
FEELINGS (BRIEFLY)?

ELABORATE AS MUCH AS YOU WISH ON ANY
TOPIC:

DAY/DATE: DAY #:

TOP FIVE FEELING WORDS FOR THIS JOURNAL
ENTRY:

WHERE AND WHAT PROMPTED THESE
FEELINGS (BRIEFLY)?

ELABORATE AS MUCH AS YOU WISH ON ANY
TOPIC:

DAY/DATE: DAY #:

TOP FIVE FEELING WORDS FOR THIS JOURNAL
ENTRY:

WHERE AND WHAT PROMPTED THESE
FEELINGS (BRIEFLY)?

ELABORATE AS MUCH AS YOU WISH ON ANY
TOPIC:

DAY/DATE: DAY #:

TOP FIVE FEELING WORDS FOR THIS JOURNAL
ENTRY:

WHERE AND WHAT PROMPTED THESE
FEELINGS (BRIEFLY)?

ELABORATE AS MUCH AS YOU WISH ON ANY
TOPIC:

DAY/DATE: DAY #:

TOP FIVE FEELING WORDS FOR THIS JOURNAL
ENTRY:

WHERE AND WHAT PROMPTED THESE
FEELINGS (BRIEFLY)?

ELABORATE AS MUCH AS YOU WISH ON ANY
TOPIC:

DAY/DATE: DAY #:

TOP FIVE FEELING WORDS FOR THIS JOURNAL
ENTRY:

WHERE AND WHAT PROMPTED THESE
FEELINGS (BRIEFLY)?

ELABORATE AS MUCH AS YOU WISH ON ANY
TOPIC:

DAY/DATE: DAY #:

TOP FIVE FEELING WORDS FOR THIS JOURNAL
ENTRY:

WHERE AND WHAT PROMPTED THESE
FEELINGS (BRIEFLY)?

ELABORATE AS MUCH AS YOU WISH ON ANY
TOPIC:

DAY/DATE: DAY #:

TOP FIVE FEELING WORDS FOR THIS JOURNAL
ENTRY:

WHERE AND WHAT PROMPTED THESE
FEELINGS (BRIEFLY)?

ELABORATE AS MUCH AS YOU WISH ON ANY
TOPIC:

DAY/DATE: DAY #:

TOP FIVE FEELING WORDS FOR THIS JOURNAL
ENTRY:

WHERE AND WHAT PROMPTED THESE
FEELINGS (BRIEFLY)?

ELABORATE AS MUCH AS YOU WISH ON ANY
TOPIC:

DAY/DATE: DAY #:

TOP FIVE FEELING WORDS FOR THIS JOURNAL
ENTRY:

WHERE AND WHAT PROMPTED THESE
FEELINGS (BRIEFLY)?

ELABORATE AS MUCH AS YOU WISH ON ANY
TOPIC:

DAY/DATE: DAY #:

TOP FIVE FEELING WORDS FOR THIS JOURNAL
ENTRY:

WHERE AND WHAT PROMPTED THESE
FEELINGS (BRIEFLY)?

ELABORATE AS MUCH AS YOU WISH ON ANY
TOPIC:

DAY/DATE: DAY #:

TOP FIVE FEELING WORDS FOR THIS JOURNAL
ENTRY:

WHERE AND WHAT PROMPTED THESE
FEELINGS (BRIEFLY)?

ELABORATE AS MUCH AS YOU WISH ON ANY
TOPIC:

DAY/DATE: DAY #:

TOP FIVE FEELING WORDS FOR THIS JOURNAL
ENTRY:

WHERE AND WHAT PROMPTED THESE
FEELINGS (BRIEFLY)?

ELABORATE AS MUCH AS YOU WISH ON ANY
TOPIC:

DAY/DATE: DAY #:

TOP FIVE FEELING WORDS FOR THIS JOURNAL
ENTRY:

WHERE AND WHAT PROMPTED THESE
FEELINGS (BRIEFLY)?

ELABORATE AS MUCH AS YOU WISH ON ANY
TOPIC:

DAY/DATE: DAY #:

TOP FIVE FEELING WORDS FOR THIS JOURNAL
ENTRY:

WHERE AND WHAT PROMPTED THESE
FEELINGS (BRIEFLY)?

ELABORATE AS MUCH AS YOU WISH ON ANY
TOPIC:

DAY/DATE: DAY #:

TOP FIVE FEELING WORDS FOR THIS JOURNAL
ENTRY:

WHERE AND WHAT PROMPTED THESE
FEELINGS (BRIEFLY)?

ELABORATE AS MUCH AS YOU WISH ON ANY
TOPIC:

DAY/DATE: DAY #:

TOP FIVE FEELING WORDS FOR THIS JOURNAL
ENTRY:

WHERE AND WHAT PROMPTED THESE
FEELINGS (BRIEFLY)?

ELABORATE AS MUCH AS YOU WISH ON ANY
TOPIC:

DAY/DATE: DAY #:

TOP FIVE FEELING WORDS FOR THIS JOURNAL
ENTRY:

WHERE AND WHAT PROMPTED THESE
FEELINGS (BRIEFLY)?

ELABORATE AS MUCH AS YOU WISH ON ANY
TOPIC:

DAY/DATE: DAY #:

TOP FIVE FEELING WORDS FOR THIS JOURNAL
ENTRY:

WHERE AND WHAT PROMPTED THESE
FEELINGS (BRIEFLY)?

ELABORATE AS MUCH AS YOU WISH ON ANY
TOPIC:

DAY/DATE: DAY #:

TOP FIVE FEELING WORDS FOR THIS JOURNAL
ENTRY:

WHERE AND WHAT PROMPTED THESE
FEELINGS (BRIEFLY)?

ELABORATE AS MUCH AS YOU WISH ON ANY
TOPIC:

DAY/DATE: DAY #:

TOP FIVE FEELING WORDS FOR THIS JOURNAL
ENTRY:

WHERE AND WHAT PROMPTED THESE
FEELINGS (BRIEFLY)?

ELABORATE AS MUCH AS YOU WISH ON ANY
TOPIC:

DAY/DATE: DAY #:

TOP FIVE FEELING WORDS FOR THIS JOURNAL
ENTRY:

WHERE AND WHAT PROMPTED THESE
FEELINGS (BRIEFLY)?

ELABORATE AS MUCH AS YOU WISH ON ANY
TOPIC:

DAY/DATE: DAY #:

TOP FIVE FEELING WORDS FOR THIS JOURNAL
ENTRY:

WHERE AND WHAT PROMPTED THESE
FEELINGS (BRIEFLY)?

ELABORATE AS MUCH AS YOU WISH ON ANY
TOPIC:

www.ingramcontent.com/pod-product-compliance
Lightning Source LLC
Chambersburg PA
CBHW070336130626
46556CB00007B/2892